D0753448

B·A·B·Y
SCiENCE

How Babies Really Work!

Ann Douglas

Illustrations by Hélène Desputeaux

Owl

To Neil and all the babies in my life.

CONTENTS

WHEN YOU Were a Baby

What were you like when you were born? Let me remind you. You were small and helpless. You couldn't talk, chew, roll over, hold a rattle, or smile. You probably couldn't even hold your head up.

Your first year of life sure was a busy one. You ate and slept. You listened and looked. You tried new things. Before your first birthday, you grew more quickly than you ever will again. And just look how you have changed! Look what you can do now!

Take a look at these babies. Watch them grow and change. You probably changed in many of the same ways.

DID YOU KNOW?

Babies grow inside their mothers' bodies for about 9 months. The unborn babies don't breathe air. They are connected to their mothers by umbilical cords. They get food and oxygen through this cord. When a baby is born — whoosh! Baby's lungs fill up for the first time.

BABY'S Body

A baby's legs may be curled up tight. Don't forget — the baby has just spent 9 months curled up inside the mother's body. Soon the baby's legs will straighten out.

Unborn babies are connected to their mothers by an umbilical cord. When a baby is born, the umbilical cord isn't needed anymore. It is cut off and tied. The short leftover stump will dry up and fall off in a week or two. Baby is left with a belly button!

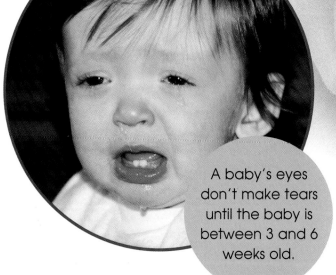

A baby's eyes don't make tears until the baby is between 3 and 6 weeks old.

A baby is born with fingernails and toenails. They grow while the baby is growing inside the mother's body. Sometimes they are so long, they need to be clipped right away!

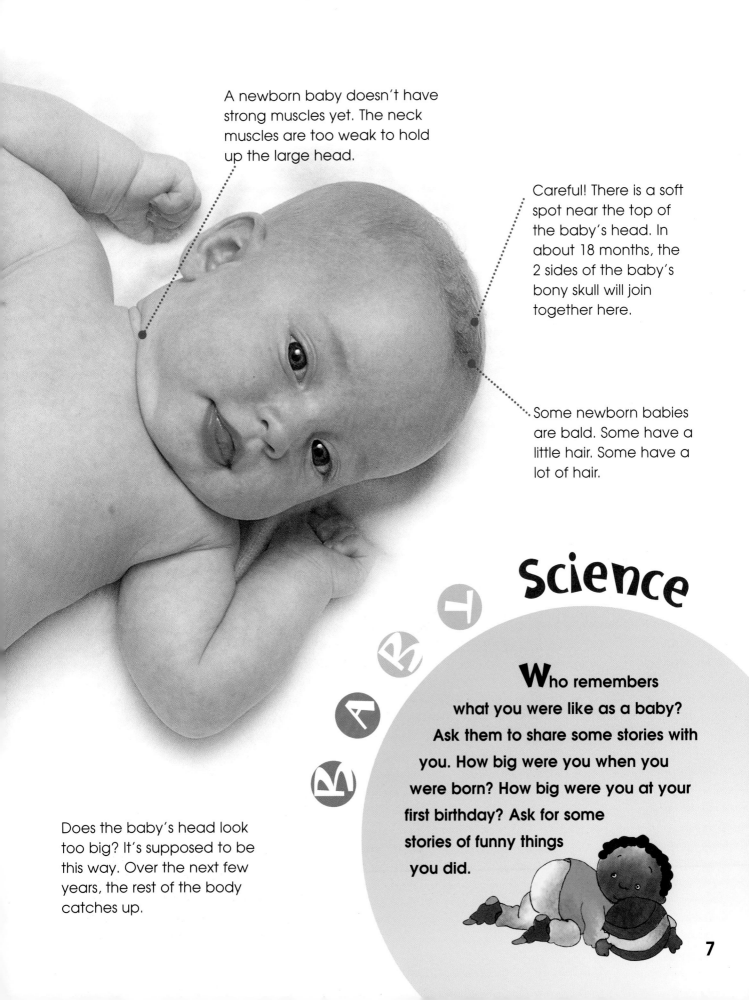

A newborn baby doesn't have strong muscles yet. The neck muscles are too weak to hold up the large head.

Careful! There is a soft spot near the top of the baby's head. In about 18 months, the 2 sides of the baby's bony skull will join together here.

Some newborn babies are bald. Some have a little hair. Some have a lot of hair.

Does the baby's head look too big? It's supposed to be this way. Over the next few years, the rest of the body catches up.

BABY Science

Who remembers what you were like as a baby? Ask them to share some stories with you. How big were you when you were born? How big were you at your first birthday? Ask for some stories of funny things you did.

7

HOLDING a Baby

Newborn babies aren't used to being in the busy, bright world. They have just spent 9 months in their mother's warm body. They felt safe curled up in that dark, quiet, small space. That's why newborn babies like being held close to another human body. They like being wrapped up in blankets. It reminds them of being curled up in Mom's body. When babies feel safe, they feel happy. They can begin to learn about their new world.

Florence is holding the baby just right. She is supporting the baby's head. The baby's neck muscles aren't strong enough to do it alone. Florence is speaking softly so she doesn't startle the baby. She is holding the baby firmly, even when the baby moves. When she is finished holding the baby, she will tell her aunt. Florence's aunt will carefully take the baby.

DID YOU KNOW?

Believe it or not, our left eye and ear are better than our right eye and ear at sensing things about feelings. Most parents naturally hold their babies on the left sides of their bodies — this brings the baby closer to their left eye and ear! Scientists think this helps the parent keep in touch with the baby's feelings. The parent knows quickly when the baby needs an extra cuddle!

MEGA-
Growing

What do newborn babies do? Some mega-growing. What helps them grow? Food and sleep. That's why newborn babies are usually only awake for short amounts of time. And when they are awake, they are usually eating.

Babies drink the same food at every meal. They drink milk from their mothers' breasts or formula from a bottle. Both types of special milk are more watery and sweeter than the milk you drink.

Sometimes babies swallow air while they are drinking their milk. The air makes the baby's stomach uncomfortable. Gently rubbing or patting the baby's back helps push the air out. Burp!

Science

Try this simple experiment. You'll find out how sweet the milk is that babies drink. Add 1 teaspoon of sugar to 3 table-spoons of warm milk. Stir until the sugar is dissolved in the milk. Now have a sip. Does it taste funny? You used to like your milk this sweet!

BABY'S
Busy Schedule

Newborn babies may eat as many as 12 meals in a day. They have to eat often because they have small stomachs. Babies may fall asleep when their stomachs are full. But in a few hours, their empty stomachs waken them again. Time to eat!

A day and a night with a newborn baby
Eat, sleep, eat, sleep — just take a look.

| Before the sun comes up | Breakfast time | Lunch time | Middle of the afternoo |

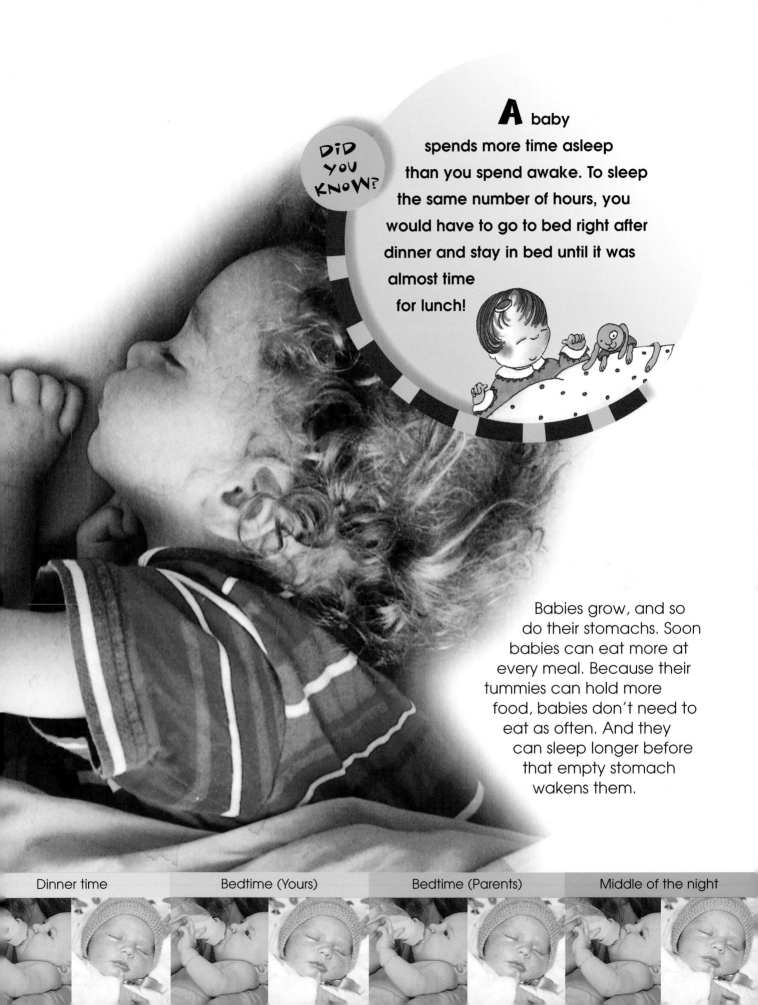

DID YOU KNOW?

A baby spends more time asleep than you spend awake. To sleep the same number of hours, you would have to go to bed right after dinner and stay in bed until it was almost time for lunch!

Babies grow, and so do their stomachs. Soon babies can eat more at every meal. Because their tummies can hold more food, babies don't need to eat as often. And they can sleep longer before that empty stomach wakens them.

Dinner time	Bedtime (Yours)	Bedtime (Parents)	Middle of the night

BABY IS Listening

As babies get older, they begin to stay awake a little more each day. They are learning more about their new world.

Babies learn a lot by listening — even before they are born. Babies have been listening from inside their mothers' bodies. It's no wonder many babies recognize their mothers' voices — and sometimes even their fathers' and brothers' and sisters' voices, too — as soon as they are born. Within a month, baby will recognize the voices of all the family members.

Watch a baby hearing a new sound. The baby may stop eating. The baby may look to see where the sound is coming from. The baby is trying to learn all about the sound.

HA!

science

Do an experiment to find out what voices babies like best. Try talking in a high, sing-song voice. Then try speaking in a very low, flat voice. What type of voice does the baby you know like best?

15

BABY IS Watching

Imagine opening your eyes to a world of light and color for the first time! That's what a newborn baby does. Do babies like looking at some things more than others? Scientists have discovered that they do. Babies enjoy looking at bright lights, strong patterns, and slowly moving objects. Most of all, babies like to look at faces!

A newborn baby can't see very far. But when you hold a baby in your arms, your face is in just the right spot. The baby's eyes can focus on your face. You can look at baby, and baby can look at you!

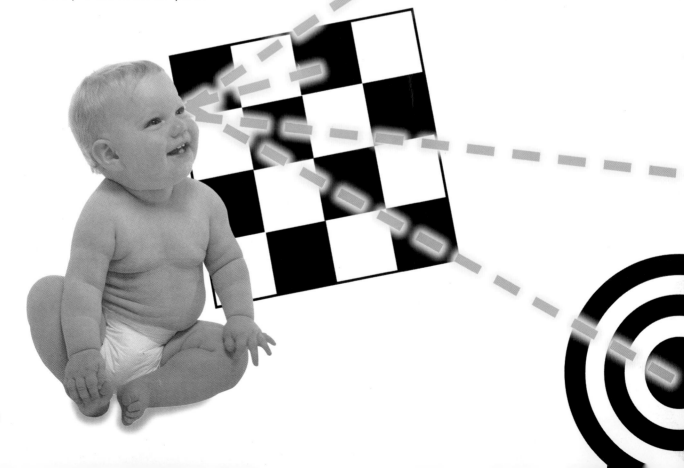

DID YOU KNOW?

Newborn babies can see black and white clearly, but they can't see colors well until they are about 4 months old. By the time babies are 2 or 3 months old, they can see objects clearly from about 3 m (6 ft) away. (That's close to the length of your bed.) By the time they are 9 months old, babies can see as far as they ever will!

HEY, That's Me!

Have you seen babies wave their arms and kick their feet? When babies are 2 or 3 months old, they discover these great toys. At first, they don't know what is making their hands and feet move. They don't know that they are part of their own bodies.

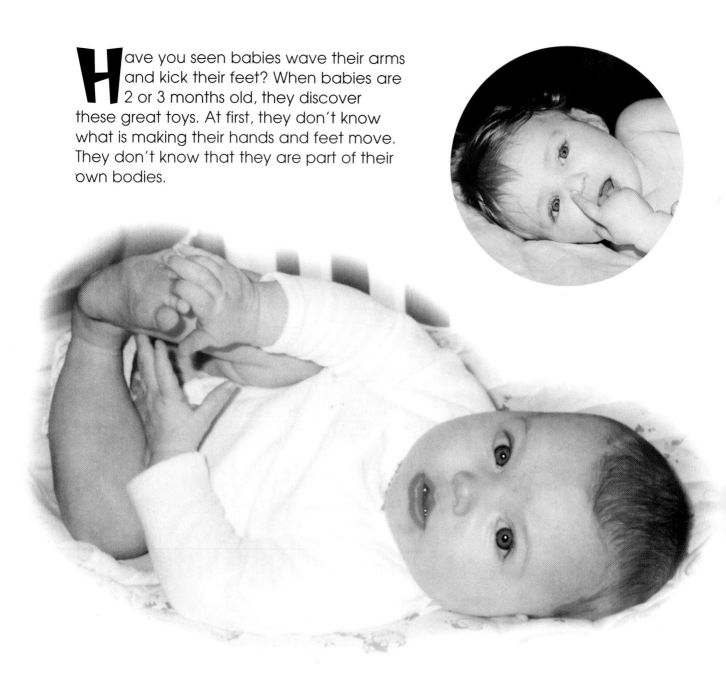

But soon babies figure it out. Then they try to pull at their fingers and clasp their hands together. Sometimes they try to shove their entire fists in their mouths. They grab their toes and suck on them.

As they use their bodies, they learn to control them. Soon babies can reach out a hand and grip a rattle. They can kick a foot to move a ball. They understand that their hands and feet belong to them. Sometime before they turn 2 years old, babies will see a surprise in the mirror. They will realize that the baby they see there isn't just another baby. "Hey, that's me!"

Science

You can control your hands really well now! So try this. Make a fist-sized hole in a large empty box. Ask a friend to place several objects in it. Reach in and touch an object. Can you use your hands alone to identify the object? Now you load up the Feely Box with objects. Let your friend have a turn!

19

BEING A Baby Detective

Babies can't talk. They can't say one single word. So how do they tell us when they are unhappy? They cry.

When babies cry, something is wrong. But what? Sometimes the answer is easy to figure out. Sometimes it isn't. A baby might cry if:
the baby is hungry
the baby is tired
the baby's diaper needs to be changed
the baby is bored
the baby needs a rest from too much excitement
the baby is too cold or too hot
the baby is lonely
the baby is sick

Trying to find out why a baby is crying can be like solving a puzzle. Because a baby can't talk, you need to use clues. You need to be a "Baby Detective." Next time you hear a baby cry, see if you can help to figure out what is wrong.

DID YOU KNOW?

Some babies cry when their diapers need to be changed. Babies wear diapers because they can't control their bladder or bowel muscles. Most babies wet their diapers 20 or 30 times a day. Having a wet or dirty diaper can be uncomfortable. It can irritate a baby's skin.

ON THE Move

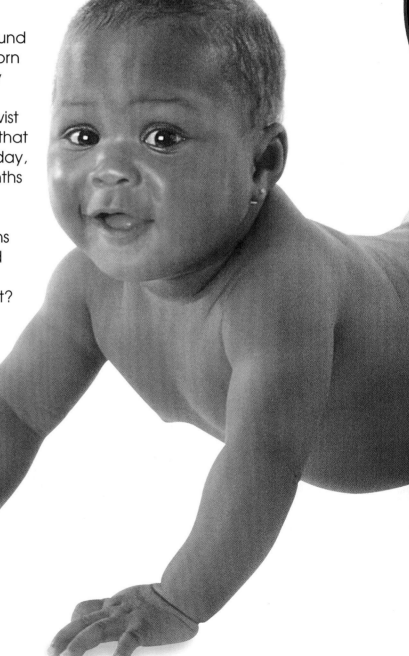

Newborns can't move around on their own. Lie a newborn on its back and it will stay there. But once babies begin to grow stronger, you'll see them twist and turn. They'll try hard to turn that heavy head and roll over. One day, when they are about 2 or 3 months old, over they go!

When babies are about 6 months old, their backs are stronger and they have better balance. They learn to sit up alone. What's next? Perhaps using those strong arms to push baby backwards across the floor. Oops — stuck under a chair again!

Some babies learn to crawl on knees and hands. Others creep on hands and feet with their bottoms sticking straight up in the air!

Science

BABY

Can you move like a baby across the room? Now see how many different ways you can use your body to move. (Don't forget rolling, hopping, tiptoeing, and sliding!)

LET'S Play!

What was your favorite game when you were a baby? Perhaps you liked looking at mobiles or listening to music. Did you laugh when someone played peek-a-boo with you? You probably enjoyed shaking rattles and squeezing a squeaky toy.

These games were fun. They taught you many things, too. Peek-a-boo showed you that someone could hide his or her face — and then appear again. You learned that when you shook the rattle or squeezed the toy, it made a noise.

When you were strong enough to sit up, you could play different games. You learned more things. You could bang spoons on lids. You could knock down towers of blocks. You could turn the pages of board books and play pat-a-cake. What a great way to learn!

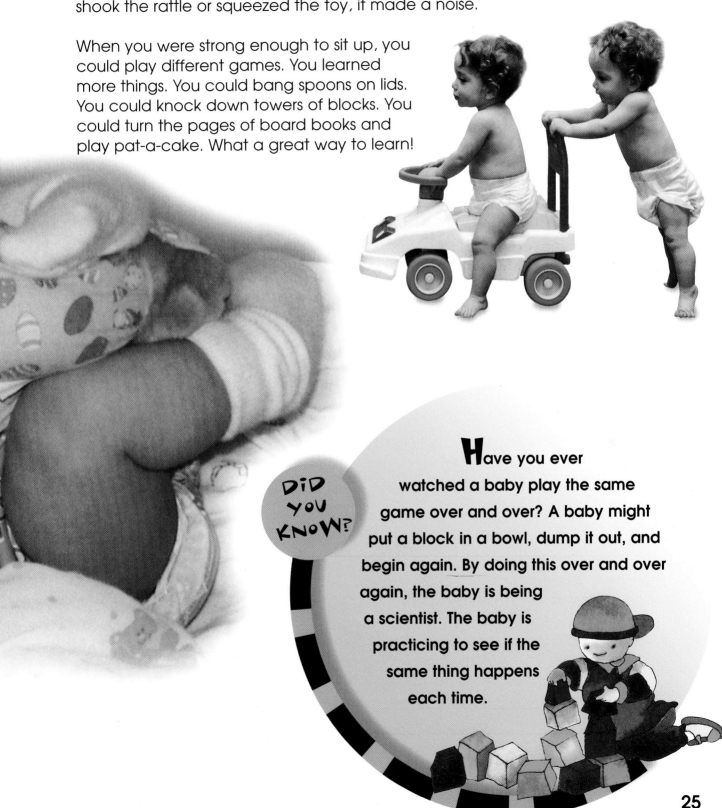

DiD YoU KNoW?

Have you ever watched a baby play the same game over and over? A baby might put a block in a bowl, dump it out, and begin again. By doing this over and over again, the baby is being a scientist. The baby is practicing to see if the same thing happens each time.

Food on a Spoon

When they are about 6 months old, babies need more than milk. Their bodies need different types of food. Now their stomachs can digest solid foods. Now they are strong enough to turn their heads away when they are full.

Six-month-old babies don't have enough teeth to chew their food. What will their first meal be? Food that is mushy or mashed, such as baby cereal or mashed potatoes. When babies learn to chew, it's time for soft food in small pieces. Bring on the macaroni, peas, and cheese cubes.

Most babies like to try to feed themselves. This is a great way for them to learn some hand control. But don't forget the bib. Whether they use a spoon or their hands, the food always seems to end up everywhere!

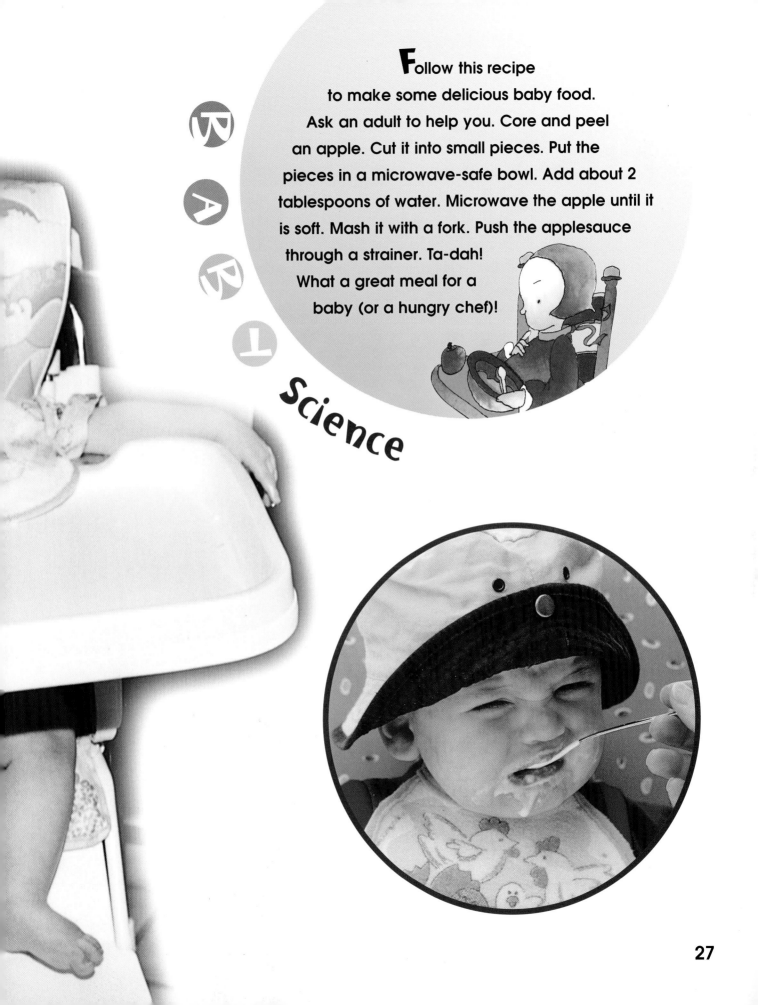

Follow this recipe to make some delicious baby food. Ask an adult to help you. Core and peel an apple. Cut it into small pieces. Put the pieces in a microwave-safe bowl. Add about 2 tablespoons of water. Microwave the apple until it is soft. Mash it with a fork. Push the applesauce through a strainer. Ta-dah! What a great meal for a baby (or a hungry chef)!

Science

FiRST Steps

Once babies learn to sit, it isn't long before they are standing. They use their hands to pull themselves up on furniture. Soon they will be holding onto the coffee table for balance. They will "cruise" from one end of it to the other.

As they practice this, babies get stronger and their balance improves. When they are about a year old, they may take a few steps by themselves. Hurray! Of course, they may fall down hard on their bottoms after taking these steps. But babies don't give up easily. They keep practicing and practicing until one day they are able to walk across an entire room.

Once babies learn how to move on their own, they can get into mischief more easily. A baby might pull a lamp off a table, pinch fingers in a drawer, or fall down a flight of stairs. Babies need someone watching them closely. Baby-watching is important work. When you are playing near a baby, do your best to help the baby stay safe.

FiRST Words

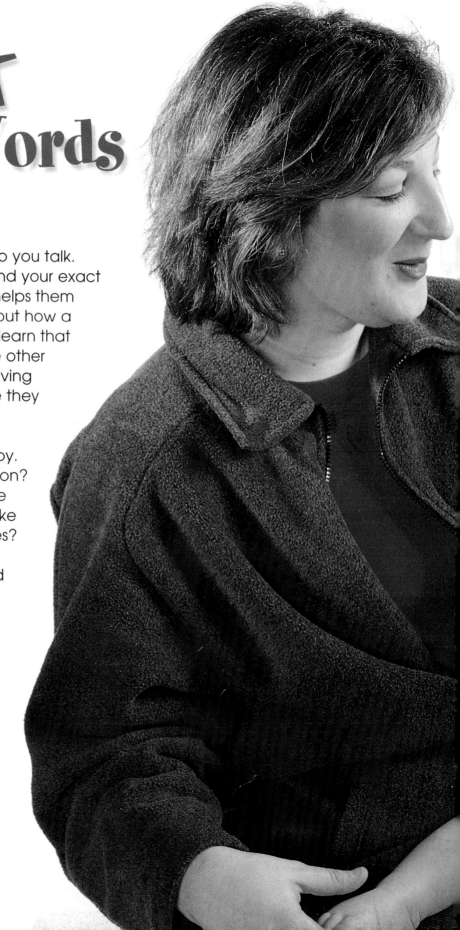

Babies love listening to you talk. They don't understand your exact words. But listening helps them learn. Babies soon figure out how a conversation works. They learn that one person talks while the other listens. Babies practice having conversations long before they learn how to say words.

Check it out: Talk to a baby. Is the baby paying attention? Now stop talking. Does the baby look at you and make cooing and gurgling noises? The baby is talking to you. If babies get really excited about the conversation, they use their whole bodies to talk. They kick their feet and wave their arms.

dadada

amama

Play a game with a friend. Think of something you want to tell the friend. Now try doing it without using any words. You can only use your body, like babies do. Here are some hints to get you started: If babies are hungry, they might crawl over to the cereal cupboard. If babies want to be picked up, they might lift their arms up in the air.

PART

Science

Babies practice making gurgling and cooing sounds. Then they try sounds like "aaaaa" and "ooooo." Next come sounds like "bababa," "dadada," and "mamama." When babies are a year old, they are usually ready to say their first real words. Maybe one of those words will be your name!

aaaaa

Owl Books are published by Greey de Pencier Books Inc.,
179 John Street, Suite 500, Toronto, Ontario M5T 3G5
The Owl colophon is a trademark of Owl Children's Trust Inc.
Greey de Pencier Books Inc. is a licensed user of trademarks of
Owl Children's Trust Inc.

Text © 1998 Ann Douglas
Illustrations © 1998 Hélène Desputeaux

All rights reserved. No part of this book may be reproduced or copied in
any form without written consent from the publisher.

Distributed in the United States by Firefly Books (U.S.) Inc.,
230 Fifth Avenue, Suite 1607, New York, NY 10001
We acknowledge the generous support of the Canada Council for the Arts
and the Ontario Arts Council for our publishing program.

Cataloguing in Publication Data
Douglas, Ann, 1963 –
Baby science: how babies really work!
ISBN 1-895688-83-3 (bound)   ISBN 1-895688-84-1 (pbk.)
1. Infants – Development – Juvenile literature. 2. Infants (Newborn) –
development – Juvenile literature. I. Title.
HQ774.D68 1998 j305.232   C97-932601-X

Design & Art Direction: **Word and Image**
Editor: **Susan Hughes**
Illustrations: **Hélène Desputeaux**

Special thanks to big kids Sam and Samantha, and to babies Adrienne,
Bram, Daniel, Emily, Felix, Florence, Ian, Jesse, Josh, Matthew, Paul, Rachel,
Sydney, and all the other truly wonderful babies in this book.

PHOTO CREDITS:
Cover, pages 1, 11 (top right), 14-15, 20-21 (center), 30-31,
back cover, Ray Boudreau; 2 (left bottom), 17, John Lewis;
2-3 (center), 22 (center), 27 (right), Image Bank; 3 (top right),
14 (bottom left), Aaron Weinstock; 3 (bottom), 12-13 (center),
19, 20 (left), 25 (top right), 26 (center), 28, 32 (top), Amy Pinchuk;
3 (top left), 32 (bottom), Sandi Meland; 4-5, 6-7 (center),
16, 23 (right), First Light; 6 (left), Diane Davy; 8, Jamie Au;
9, 20 (right), 29 (bottom), Bill Lau; 10-11 (center), 12-13
(baby with bottle), 29 (top), Tony Stone; 12-13 (sleeping baby),
Tracey Brooks Jacklin; 18 (bottom), Arnold Winterhoff;
18 (top), Carolyn Meland; 23 (top left), 24-25 (center),
Josephine Cheng.

Printed in Hong Kong
A B C D E F